Could You Love Me Like My God

BETH FOWLER

A FIRESIDE BOOK PUBLISHED BY SIMON & SCHUSTER

F I R E S I D E
Rockefeller Center
1230 Avenue of the Americas
New York, NY 10020

Copyright © 1997 by Beth Fowler

FIRESIDE and colophon are registered trademarks of Simon & Schuster Inc.

Beth Fowler is the owner of the trademark "COULD YOU LOVE ME LIKE MY™".

Designed & illustrated by Jill Weber

Manufactured in the United States of America

1 3 5 7 9 10 8 6 4 2

Library of Congress Cataloging-in-Publication Data is available.

ISBN 0-684-83844-3

Have you ever been so blessed,
you felt you could never thank God enough?

I have. It was when I first came to know God,
and since then, I've felt blessed time after time,
day after day, more than I can count.

 Thank You, God, for my life with You
and for always showing me the way.

Dedicated to my friend Misty,
whose love and creativity
serve as messengers to many

Blessings and thanks to those who lit my way to God:
Liz Bremond, Mary Jayne and Bruce Fogerty, Helen and
Frank Stevenson, and Jay Turner, and to those who made
this book possible: my family, Dave, Mark, Carolyn, Scott,
Louise, and especially, Laurie, whose insight and
many contributions shone with inspiration.

Could you reassure me that
we'll always be together?

$\mathscr{C}$ould you send someone to intercede for me
when I can't find the words?

Could you speak to me from my heart?

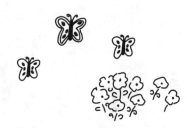

Could you always be glad to hear from me,
no matter how long it's been?

$\mathscr{C}$ould you always forgive me?

*C*ould you show yourself in
almost every face I see?

Could you visit me in my dreams?

*C*ould you help me overcome
my shortcomings?

*C*ould you encourage me?

Could you teach me how to love?

*C*ould you always accept me, especially
when I can't accept myself?

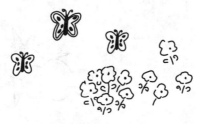

$\mathcal{C}$ould you let me know when I'm on track
with a little flutter in my heart?

$\mathcal{C}$ould you be with me in spirit?

*C*ould you make me tremble?

*C*ould you share your wisdom?

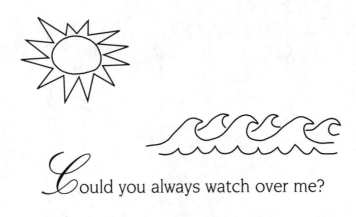

Could you always watch over me?

*C*ould you never stop calling me?

*C*ould you always be full of surprises?

*C*ould you pave the way for my
hopes and dreams?

Could you send me secret gifts?

*C*ould you take me on adventures?

Could you travel everywhere with me?

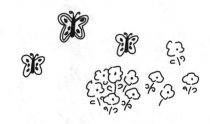

*C*ould you show me that you know best?

Could you provide new ways
to see and hear you?

Could you guide me from within?

*C*ould you turn my burdens into wings?

Could you pull me out when I fall
into a deep, dark pit?

31

Could you take away my fear?

*C*ould you always delight in me?

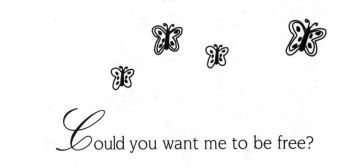

$\mathscr{C}$ould you want me to be free?

*C*ould you ask only for my love?

$\mathcal{C}$ould you change my heart?

$\mathscr{C}$ould you not mind if I tell others
how wonderful you are?

Could you accept my adoration?

Could you guide me whenever I am lost?

*C*ould you give me strength when I feel weak?

_C_ould you always hear me say your name?

*C*ould you let me know what pleases you?

Could you be steadfast in your love
so that it endures forever?

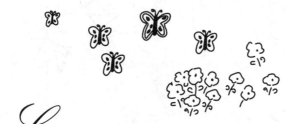

$\mathscr{C}$ould you help me be more like you?

$\mathcal{C}$ould you hold me in your arms?

Could you be the spring inside me
that lets me dance for you?

Could you always have compassion?

*C*ould you save me a place to sit beside you?

Could you be faithful?

Could you like it when I sing to you?

$\mathcal{C}$ould you always speak the truth?

$\mathcal{C}$ould you know my thoughts
before I even think them?

Could you call to me from the wind?

$\mathcal{C}$ould you enjoy sharing peace and quiet?

*C*ould you fill me when I'm out of breath?

Could you always be my shield?

$\mathcal{C}$ould you heal my hurts and wounds?

*C*ould you turn my sadness into laughter?

*C*ould you always be glad to help?

Could you make me sure that with you
there's nothing I can't do?

$\mathcal{C}$ould you never leave me?

Could you always be a blessing?

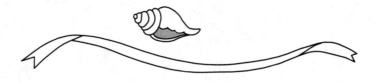

Could you save me from myself?

Could you catch me when I slip?

$\mathcal{C}$ould you be my stronghold in times of trouble?

*C*ould you reward me more than I deserve?

$\mathscr{C}$ould you always be concerned about me?

*C*ould you be my resting place?

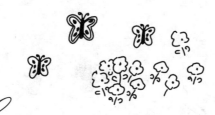

Could you teach me to ask you
for whatever it is I need?

*C*ould you always melt my heart?

$\mathcal{C}$ould you trust me to do things for you?

*C*ould you teach me to soar with you and
not be afraid of heights?

Could you always set the table?

*C*ould you show me the light?

*C*ould you fill my cup so full it's always overflowing?

$\mathscr{C}$ould you assure me that you're on your way,
so it's easier to wait for you?

Could you bring me joy?

*C*ould you always have room
in your house for me?

Could you quench my thirst?

Could you not mind when I need you?

*C*ould you offer me everything you have?

*C*ould you be full of grace?

$\mathscr{C}$ould you let me know I am precious to you?

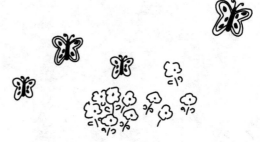

*C*ould you have a mighty arm and strong hand
when I lean on you?

*C*ould you always keep your promises?

*C*ould you not mind when I pour out
my heart to you?

*C*ould you be my fortress when things
don't go my way?

Could you carry me when I'm too tired?

$\mathscr{C}$ould you never be too busy to counsel me?

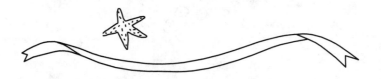

*C*ould you never shame me?

Could you establish the work that I'm to do?

Could you always cover for me?

$\mathcal{C}$ould you never break your word?

*C*ould you honor me?

$\mathcal{C}$ould you send me guardian angels?

*C*ould you show me beauty?

*C*ould you provide signs and clues
so I better understand you?

Could you always console and cheer me?

*C*ould you be my shepherd?

Could you protect me?

$\mathcal{C}$ould you give me an open invitation
to always seek you out?

*C*ould you show me many wonders?

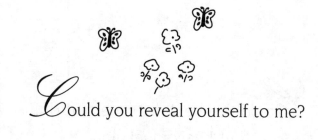

*C*ould you reveal yourself to me?

*C*ould you be so much a part of me
that I never feel alone?

*C*ould you always inspire me?

Could you appreciate everything I offer you?

Could you swim with me in the deep?

*C*ould you clothe me in regal garments?

_C_ould you never cease to amaze me?

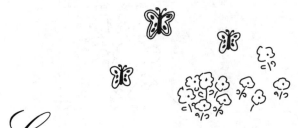

$\mathcal{C}$ould you be there if I make a leap of faith?

*C*ould you never turn away when I need you?

*C*ould you be merciful?

Could you make yourself available to all,
no matter how great or small they are?

*C*ould you enlarge my understanding
of many mysteries?

Could you be my refuge from the world?

*C*ould you always give me hope?

*C*ould you say things to me that are sweeter than honey?

*C*ould you delight me?

*C*ould you calm and quiet my soul?

*C*ould you open doors and gates for me?

*C*ould you let me abide in you?

*C*ould you become acquainted with all my ways?

$\mathcal{C}$ould you search out a path for me?

$\mathcal{C}$ould you always know what I'm about to say?

Could you share your thoughts?

*C*ould you never turn away from me?

*C*ould you lift me up when I'm bowed down?

*C*ould you always be nearby?

$\mathcal{C}$ould you show me things
I've never seen before?

*C*ould you gently lay your hand on me?

$\mathcal{C}$ould you mend my broken heart?

$\mathscr{C}$ould you give me a ride when I can't walk?

Could you know the plan for me to prosper?

*C*ould you transform my life?

*C*ould you gaze at me with a shining face?

*C*ould you claim me as your own?

Could you whisper softly to me?

Could you be glad to meet me on short notice
anytime, anywhere?

*C*ould you create a wonderful life
for us together?

Could you show me how much fun it is to give?

$\mathcal{C}$ould you be my foundation?

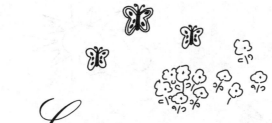

*C*ould you understand me as if
you'd walked in my shoes?

$\mathcal{C}$ould you be the answer to my prayers?

$\mathcal{C}$ould you never ignore me?

Could you see me as the apple of your eye?

Could you move the earth for me?

*C*ould you receive and help anyone
I send to you?

Could you always hold out your hand to me?

Could you lead me when I go wandering?

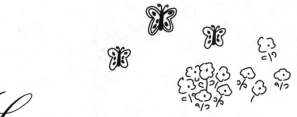

Could you prove to me over and over how much I can entrust to you?

*C*ould you have a sense of humor?

*C*ould you part the sea for me?

$\mathcal{C}$ould you comfort me?

*C*ould you teach me humility?

$\mathcal{C}$ould you treasure the gifts I bring you?

Could you enlighten me?

*C*ould you be the star of my life?

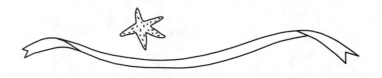

$\mathcal{C}$ould you bring me the rainbow?

$\mathscr{C}$ould you long for me as much
as I long for you?

*C*ould you promise to spend eternity with me?